THIS BOOK BELONGS TO

Vicky Rasinske

No protion of this book may be reproduced in whole or in part shared with others, stored in a retriveal system, digitized or transmitted in any from without written persission from the author.

COLOR TEST

Basic tips of Drawing!

- ★ A little bit of art theory is always good to know, Lets start........

- ★ All you need is a pencil,eraser and a piece off paper!

- ★ Draw lightly at first because you might need to erase some lines as you work.

- ★ Add details according to the diagrams but dont worry about being perfect. Artists frequently make mistakes they just find ways to make their mistakes look interesting.

- ★ Dont worry if your drawing dont turn out the way you want them to , just keep practicing ! Sometimes drawing the same thing just a few times will help.

- ★ Once you have finished your drawing in pencil you can trace it with a black fineliner pen and color or paint it to your liking.

Turn the page for some cool composition ideas!!!

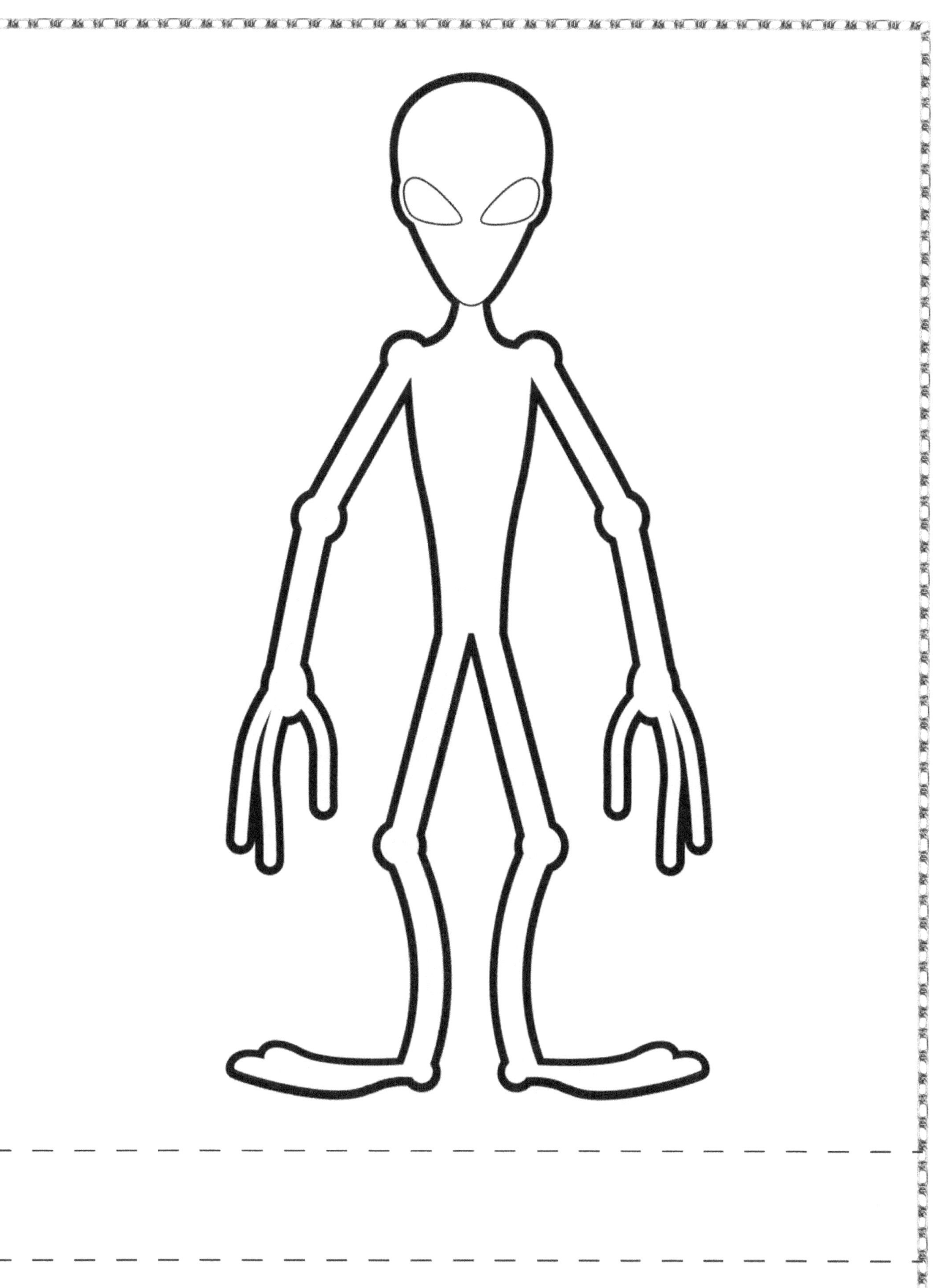

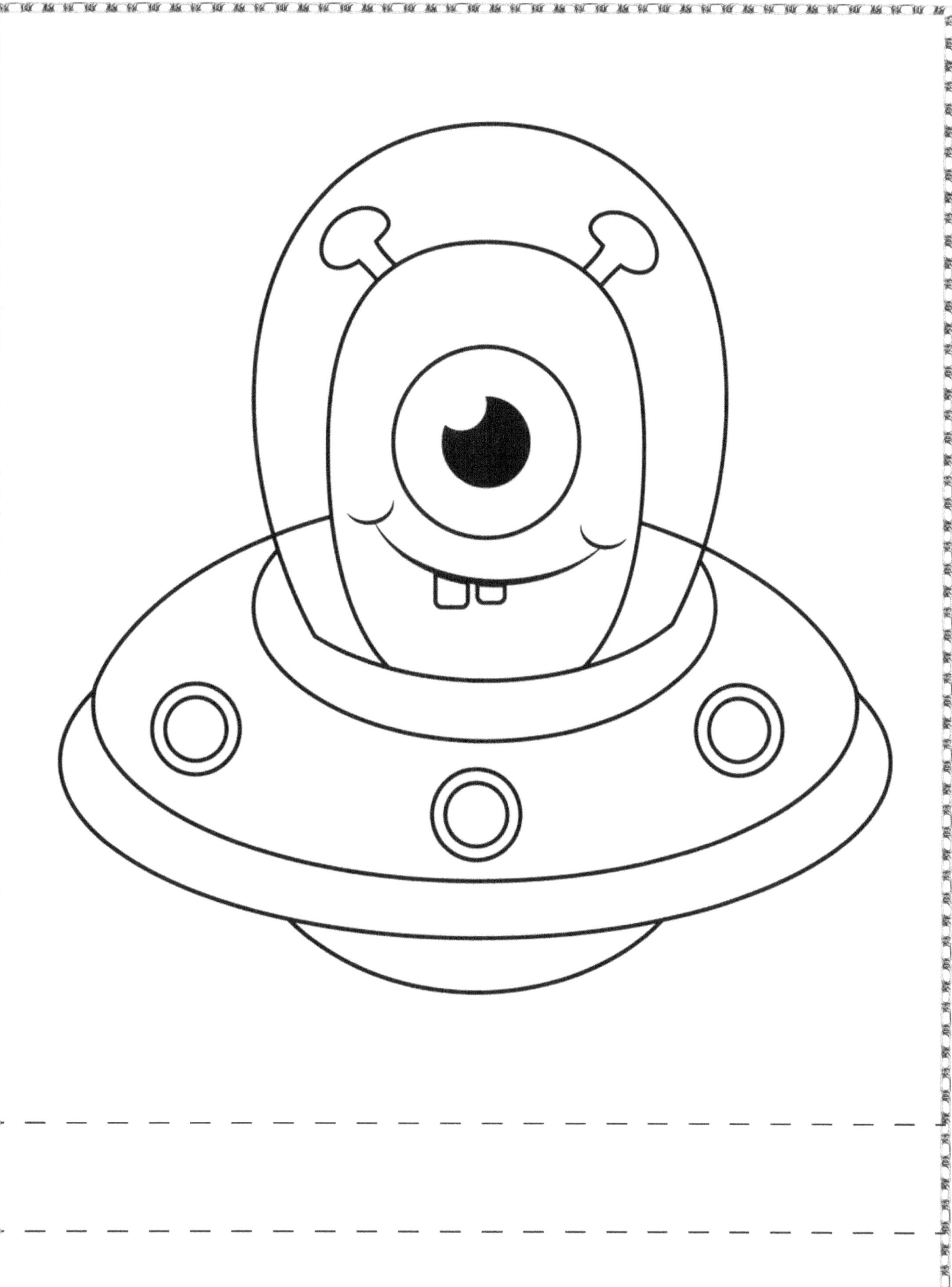

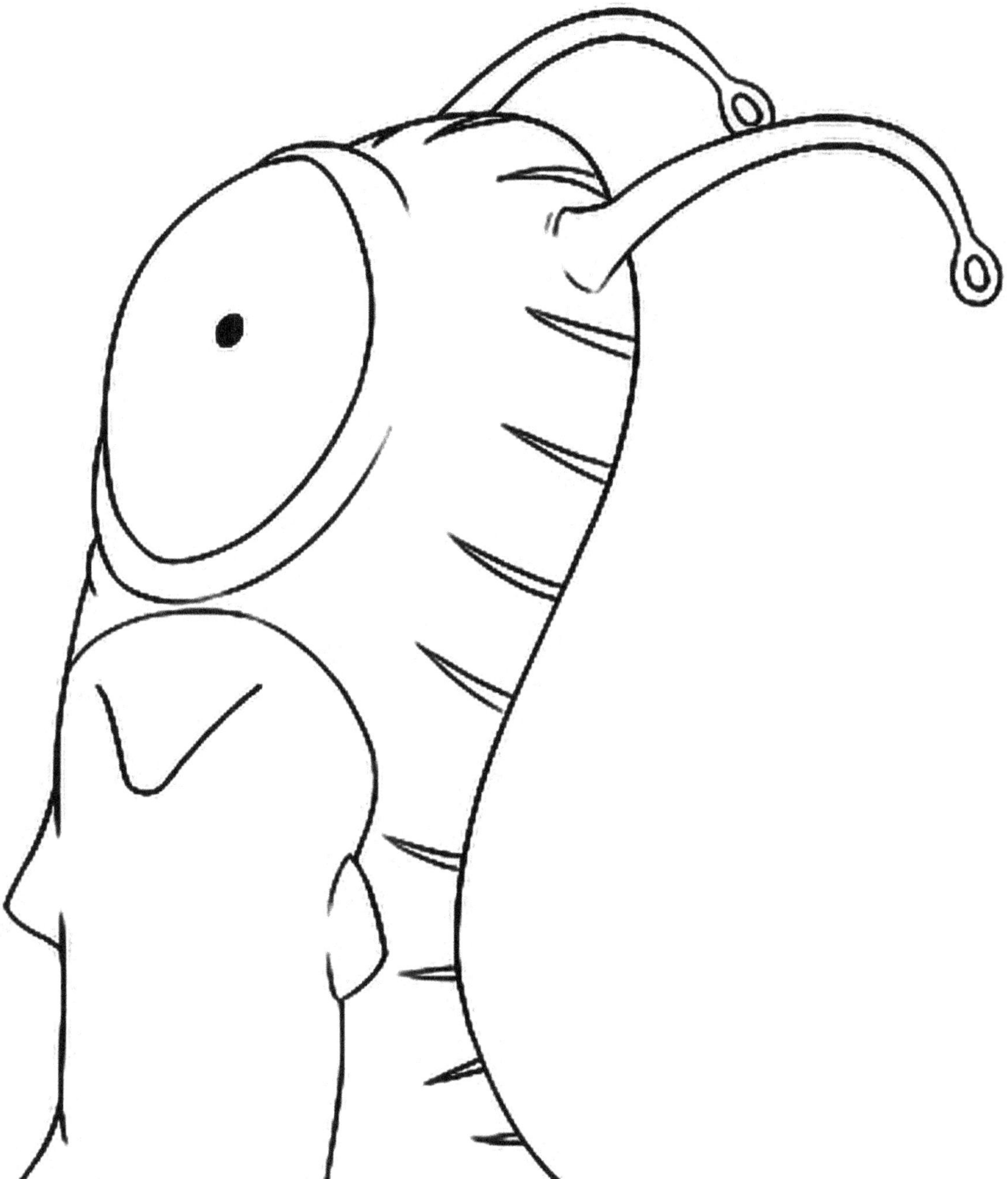